SEATTLE SEAHAWKS

BRENDAN FLYNN

WWW.APEXEDITIONS.COM

Copyright © 2025 by Apex Editions, Mendota Heights, MN 55120. All rights reserved. No part of this book may be reproduced or utilized in any form or by any means without written permission from the publisher.

Apex is distributed by North Star Editions:
sales@northstareditions.com | 888-417-0195

Produced for Apex by Red Line Editorial.

Photographs ©: Lindsey Wasson/AP Images, cover, 1; Kirby Lee/Getty Images Sport/Getty Images, 4–5; Abbie Parr/AP Images, 6–7; Vernon Biever/AP Images, 8–9; Bill Smith/Getty Images Sport/Getty Images, 10–11; Al Messerschmidt/AP Images, 12–13; Doug Pensinger/Allsport/Getty Images Sport/Getty Images, 14–15; Harry How/Getty Images Sport/Getty Images, 16–17; David Durochik/AP Images, 19; George Gojkovich/Getty Images Sport/Getty Images, 20–21; Tim DeFrisco/Getty Images Sport/Getty Images, 22–23; Rick Stewart/Getty Images Sport/Getty Images, 24–25; Kevin Casey/NFLPhotoLibrary/Getty Images Sport/Getty Images, 26–27; Scott Halleran/Allsport/Getty Images Sport/Getty Images, 29; Otto Greule Jr./Getty Images Sport/Getty Images, 30–31, 40–41, 54–55; Jeff Gross/Getty Images Sport/Getty Images, 32–33, 52–53; Christian Petersen/Getty Images Sport/Getty Images, 34–35; Justin Casterline/Getty Images Sport/Getty Images, 36–37; Stephen Brashear/AP Images, 39, 57; Jason Miller/Getty Images Sport/Getty Images, 42–43; Scott Halleran/Getty Images Sport/Getty Images, 44–45; Jonathan Ferrey/Getty Images Sport/Getty Images, 46–47; Shutterstock Images, 48–49, 50–51, 58–59

Library of Congress Control Number: 2024939368

ISBN
979-8-89250-159-0 (hardcover)
979-8-89250-176-7 (paperback)
979-8-89250-300-6 (ebook pdf)
979-8-89250-193-4 (hosted ebook)

Printed in the United States of America
Mankato, MN
012025

NOTE TO PARENTS AND EDUCATORS

Apex books are designed to build literacy skills in striving readers. Exciting, high-interest content attracts and holds readers' attention. The text is carefully leveled to allow students to achieve success quickly.

TABLE OF CONTENTS

CHAPTER 1
THE 12TH MAN 4

CHAPTER 2
EARLY HISTORY 8

PLAYER SPOTLIGHT
STEVE LARGENT 18

CHAPTER 3
LEGENDS 20

PLAYER SPOTLIGHT
CORTEZ KENNEDY 28

CHAPTER 4
RECENT HISTORY 30

PLAYER SPOTLIGHT
RUSSELL WILSON 38

CHAPTER 5
MODERN STARS 40

CHAPTER 6
TEAM TRIVIA 48

TEAM RECORDS • 56
TIMELINE • 58
COMPREHENSION QUESTIONS • 60
GLOSSARY • 62
TO LEARN MORE • 63
ABOUT THE AUTHOR • 63
INDEX • 64

CHAPTER 1

THE 12TH MAN

Thousands of fans walk through downtown Seattle, Washington. They're wearing blue and green gear. They talk excitedly about the Seahawks. The fans enter the stadium. It's game day!

The Seattle Seahawks have some of the loudest fans in the NFL.

The fans roar as the home team runs onto the field. They get louder as the game goes on. Every big play sends them into a frenzy. The stands seem to shake as the Seahawks score another touchdown. The Seahawks roll to a big win!

HONORING THE FANS
The Seattle Seahawks retired jersey No. 12 in honor of their fans. The crowd in Seattle is often referred to as the 12th Man. They make so much noise that it feels as if the Seahawks have an extra player on the field.

Seattle safety Quandre Diggs (23) celebrates with his teammates after a big play.

CHAPTER 2

EARLY HISTORY

The Seattle Seahawks entered the NFL in 1976. They were an expansion team. They joined the same year as the Tampa Bay Buccaneers. The Seahawks struggled in their first year. They won only two games.

Quarterback Jim Zorn (10) looks for a receiver during a 1976 game against the Green Bay Packers.

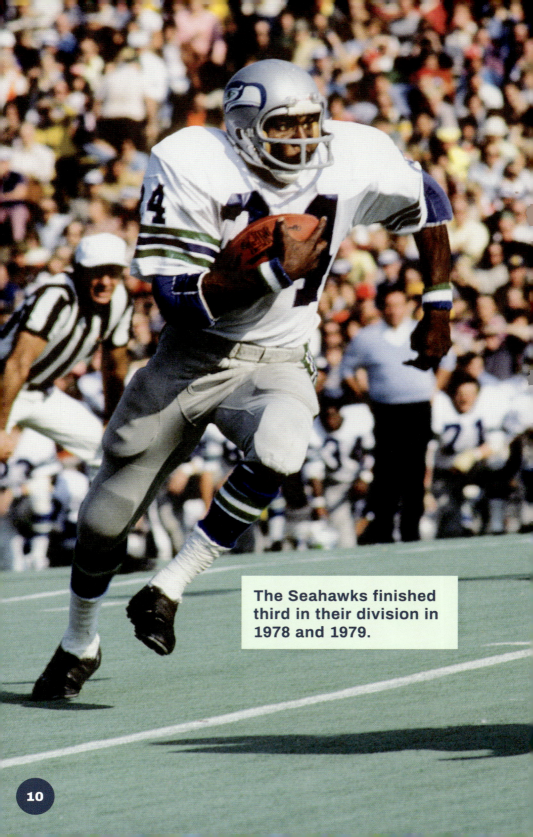

The Seahawks finished third in their division in 1978 and 1979.

It didn't take long for the Seahawks to improve. They finished 9–7 in both 1978 and 1979. However, Seattle was in a strong division. The Seahawks didn't reach the playoffs in either season.

WELCOME BACK

The Seahawks played their first year in the NFC West Division. The next year, they moved to the AFC West. They stayed there for more than 30 years. In 2002, the NFL changed its divisions. Seattle returned to the NFC West.

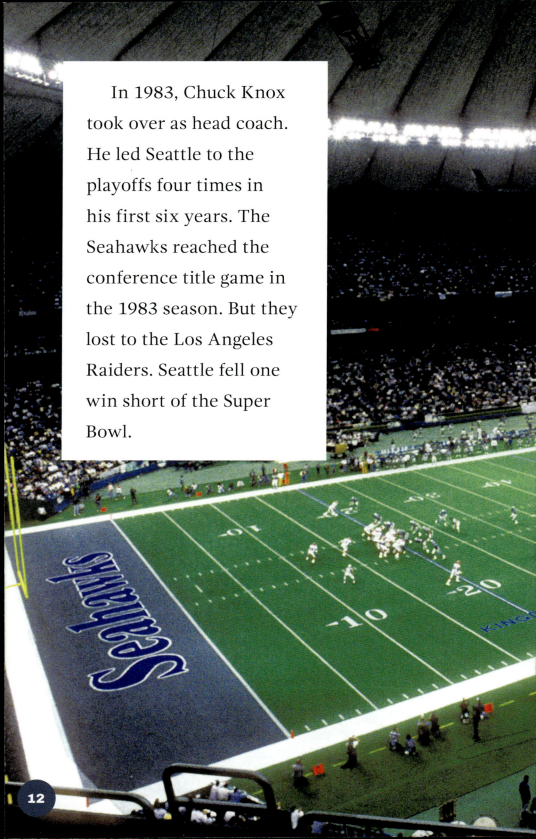

In 1983, Chuck Knox took over as head coach. He led Seattle to the playoffs four times in his first six years. The Seahawks reached the conference title game in the 1983 season. But they lost to the Los Angeles Raiders. Seattle fell one win short of the Super Bowl.

THE KINGDOME

The Seattle Kingdome was the Seahawks' first home stadium. The team played there from 1976 to 1999. The building's concrete roof was the largest of any stadium in the world.

The Kingdome could seat more than 65,000 fans.

The Seahawks began a rough stretch in 1989. They went 10 years without reaching the playoffs. Then in 1999, the team hired Mike Holmgren as head coach. He helped turn things around. Holmgren led Seattle to a division title in his first season.

HOME AWAY FROM HOME

In 1994, the Kingdome needed repairs. Then in 2000 and 2001, the Seahawks were building a new stadium. Both times, the Seahawks found a home at the University of Washington. They played at Husky Stadium.

Mike Holmgren (right) talks with quarterback Matt Hasselbeck (8) during a 2001 game.

Under Holmgren, the Seahawks became winners. They reached the playoffs every year from 2003 to 2007. Their best season came in 2005. They went 13–3. Then they made it to the Super Bowl for the first time. However, Seattle lost to the Pittsburgh Steelers. It was a controversial game. The officials later admitted to mistakes that hurt the Seahawks. It was a tough way to lose.

The Seahawks destroyed the Carolina Panthers 34–14 in the conference championship game to reach their first Super Bowl.

PLAYER SPOTLIGHT

STEVE LARGENT

Steve Largent wasn't blessed with great speed or size. But he played with extreme focus. And he prepared more than most. He also caught nearly everything thrown in his direction.

STEVE LARGENT HAD MORE THAN 13,000 CAREER RECEIVING YARDS.

Largent was a rookie in 1976. That was the Seahawks' first season. Largent stuck with Seattle until he retired in 1989. At the time, he held most NFL career receiving records. Largent became the first player with 100 touchdown catches. He also caught at least one pass in 177 straight games.

CHAPTER 3

LEGENDS

Jim Zorn served as Seattle's quarterback for the team's first eight seasons. He became known for scrambling. Dave Krieg took over for Zorn in the middle of the 1983 season. Both Zorn and Krieg connected with Steve Largent on many huge plays.

Jim Zorn threw for a career-high 3,661 yards during the 1979 season.

Curt Warner led Seattle's running game in the 1980s. Warner ran for 1,449 yards as a rookie in 1983. The next year, he had a bad knee injury. Experts thought his career might be over. But Warner came back strong. He topped 1,000 rushing yards in three of the next four seasons. That included a career-high 1,481 yards in 1986. Warner also scored 13 touchdowns that season.

Curt Warner (28) dodges a defender during a 1988 game against the Los Angeles Raiders.

Defensive tackle Cortez Kennedy was the face of the Seahawks in the 1990s. But Seattle had many defensive standouts. Dave Brown pulled down 50 career interceptions. That's a Seahawks record. Safety Kenny Easley was one of the NFL's hardest hitters. He nabbed 10 interceptions in 1984. That led the NFL.

SACK MASTER

Jacob Green started at left defensive end from 1980 to 1991. During his last 10 years, he recorded 97.5 sacks. Only two NFL players had more. Green joined Seattle's Ring of Honor in 1995.

In 1984, Kenny Easley earned the Defensive Player of the Year Award.

25

Shaun Alexander topped 1,000 rushing yards five years in a row.

Running back Shaun Alexander burst onto the scene in 2001. He led the NFL with 14 rushing touchdowns. He earned the NFL Most Valuable Player Award in 2005. His 1,880 yards and 27 touchdowns led the league.

Left tackle Walter Jones opened huge running lanes for Alexander. Jones was a nine-time Pro Bowl pick.

SUPER BOWL QB

Matt Hasselbeck joined the Seahawks in 2001. He was their starting quarterback for the next 10 years. Hasselbeck became the first Seahawks quarterback to lead the team to the Super Bowl.

PLAYER SPOTLIGHT

CORTEZ KENNEDY

The Seahawks had the third overall pick in 1990. They drafted defensive tackle Cortez Kennedy. He anchored the defensive line for 11 seasons. Kennedy earned the Defensive Player of the Year Award in his third season. He tallied 14 sacks that season. That was more than any other interior lineman.

Kennedy often fought off double teams. But he still made huge plays. Kennedy entered the Pro Football Hall of Fame in 2012.

CORTEZ KENNEDY MADE EIGHT PRO BOWLS IN HIS CAREER.

CHAPTER 4

RECENT HISTORY

The Seahawks made a coaching change in 2010. Pete Carroll stepped in. Carroll had won two national titles at the University of Southern California. It didn't take long for him to have an impact in Seattle. Carroll led the Seahawks to the playoffs in his first season.

Pete Carroll cheers during a playoff game in the 2010 season.

Rookie quarterback Russell Wilson took over in 2012. The next season, Seattle went 13–3. That was the best record in the conference. The Seahawks pulled off two close playoff wins. In the Super Bowl, they faced the Denver Broncos. Seattle crushed Denver 43–8.

LEGION OF BOOM

Seattle's secondary earned the nickname the "Legion of Boom" during their Super Bowl run. The team's defensive backs shut down opposing receivers. And they put big hits on anyone who had the ball.

Malcolm Smith (53) ran back an interception for a touchdown during the Super Bowl.

In the 2014 season, Jermaine Kearse (15) caught a touchdown in overtime to win the conference title and advance to the Super Bowl.

Seattle returned to the Super Bowl in the 2014 season. The team faced the New England Patriots. The Seahawks trailed by four points late in the game. Then Wilson led a long drive. Seattle had the ball on New England's 1-yard line. Only 26 seconds were left. But Wilson threw an interception. The Patriots won.

BRRRRRR!

In the 2015 season, the Seahawks visited the Minnesota Vikings in the playoffs. It was one of the coldest games in NFL history. The wind chill was minus 25 degrees Fahrenheit (−32°C). Seattle scored 10 points in the fourth quarter. They beat the Vikings 10–9.

In 2021, wide receiver Tyler Lockett recorded 1,175 receiving yards.

Wilson led the Seahawks to the playoffs four more times in his last six seasons with the team. But Seattle never made it past the second round. In 2022, a big trade shocked the NFL. The Seahawks sent Wilson to the Broncos. Geno Smith took over at quarterback for Seattle. He led the team to winning records in each of his first two seasons.

PLAYER SPOTLIGHT

RUSSELL WILSON

Quarterback Russell Wilson wasn't supposed to be Seattle's starter in his rookie season. But he impressed the coaches in the preseason. He won the job.

Wilson led the Seahawks for 10 years. He didn't miss a start during his first nine seasons. The team averaged 10 wins per year under Wilson. And he was named to the Pro Bowl nine times. Wilson was short for a quarterback. But he used his quick feet to keep plays alive. Wilson had a strong arm, too. He topped 4,000 passing yards four times.

WILSON THREW 292 TOUCHDOWN PASSES WITH THE SEAHAWKS.

CHAPTER 5

MODERN STARS

Russell Wilson was a surprise as a rookie. He quickly became one of the NFL's top quarterbacks. Running back Marshawn Lynch was another key part of Seattle's Super Bowl teams. He pounded defenses with his hard-nosed runs.

Marshawn Lynch carries the ball during a 2011 game.

D. K. Metcalf averaged more than 1,000 receiving yards per season in his first five years in Seattle.

Wilson had a couple of favorite targets. One was wide receiver Tyler Lockett. He often stayed under the radar. But he steadily scored touchdowns year after year. Then D. K. Metcalf arrived as a rookie in 2019. He had an elite blend of size and speed.

WALKER, THE RUNNER

Kenneth Walker III won the starting running back job in 2022. It was his rookie season. Walker ran for 1,050 yards that year. He also scored nine touchdowns. Walker nearly matched those numbers in 2023.

43

Richard Sherman returns an interception for a touchdown in a 2013 game.

The Legion of Boom had a few key players. Richard Sherman recorded eight interceptions in 2013. That led the NFL. At safety, Earl Thomas and Kam Chancellor were a dynamic duo. Thomas earned six Pro Bowl nods with the Seahawks. Chancellor earned four.

SURPRISE PICK

Riq Woolen was a pleasant surprise in 2022. Seattle drafted the cornerback in the fifth round. Then he led the NFL with six interceptions that season.

Few linebackers have been more dominant than Bobby Wagner. He splashed onto the scene as a rookie in 2012. He racked up a team-high 140 tackles. Wagner went on to lead the league in tackles three times. In 2023, he tallied a career-high 183 tackles.

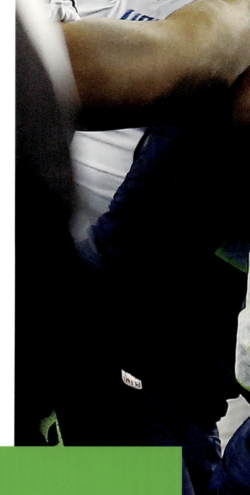

STAR SAFETY

Safety Quandre Diggs began his career with the Detroit Lions. But he joined the Seahawks in 2019. He made a huge impact. Diggs started every game the next four years. In 2020, he made the first of three straight Pro Bowls.

In 2016, Bobby Wagner (54) made a league-leading 167 tackles.

CHAPTER 6

TEAM TRIVIA

The seahawk isn't a real bird. The name may have been inspired by ospreys and seagulls. The team's logo is based on a ceremonial mask. The Kwakwaka'wakw (kwock-KWOCKY-wowk) carved it. These Indigenous people live in the Pacific Northwest.

Birds form an important part of Kwakwaka'wakw culture.

Seattle is not the first city with a pro football team called the Seahawks. In 1946, the AAFC formed. This league was a rival to the NFL. One of its teams was the Miami Seahawks.

Both Seattle (pictured) and Miami, Florida, are located along the ocean.

OTHER NAMES

In 1975, the owners of Seattle's new football team held a naming contest. More than 100 fans suggested Seahawks. Other ideas included Sockeyes, Mariners, Olympics, and Evergreens.

Jerry Rice runs with the ball during a 2004 game with the Seahawks.

The Seahawks retired Steve Largent's jersey in 1992. He wore No. 80. But in 2004, wide receiver Jerry Rice joined the team. Rice had worn No. 80 all through his amazing career. Largent agreed to let Rice wear No. 80. Rice played 11 games with the Seahawks. Then he retired the next summer.

During the "Beast Quake," Marshawn Lynch (24) ran for 67 yards.

The "Beast Quake" is a legendary play in NFL history. Seattle hosted New Orleans in the 2010 playoffs. Marshawn Lynch took a handoff. He zigzagged through the defense. He broke many tackles. Then Lynch leaped into the end zone. The crowd erupted. A scientist checked a seismograph. The fans' jumping had shown up as a small earthquake!

LOUD CROWD

Seahawks fans know how to make noise. In a 2005 game, their noise forced 11 false-start penalties. In 2013, the crowd set a world record for crowd noise at a game. Fans cheered louder than a jet engine on takeoff.

TEAM RECORDS

All-Time Passing Yards: 37,059
Russell Wilson (2012–21)

All-Time Touchdown Passes: 292
Russell Wilson (2012–21)

All-Time Rushing Yards: 9,429
Shaun Alexander (2000–07)

All-Time Rushing Touchdowns: 100
Shaun Alexander (2000–07)

All-Time Receiving Yards: 13,089
Steve Largent (1976–89)

All-Time Interceptions: 50
Dave Brown (1976–86)

All-Time Sacks: 115.5*
Jacob Green (1980–91)

All-Time Scoring: 810
Norm Johnson (1982–90)

All-Time Coaching Wins: 137
Pete Carroll (2010–23)

Super Bowl Titles: 1
(2013)

Sacks were not an official statistic until 1982. However, researchers have studied old games to determine sacks dating back to 1960.

All statistics are accurate through 2023.

TIMELINE

1976 — The Seattle Seahawks go 2–12 in their first NFL season.

1983 — New head coach Chuck Knox leads the Seahawks to the playoffs for the first time.

1999 — The Seahawks win the division in their first year under head coach Mike Holmgren.

2002 — The Seahawks open their new stadium in downtown Seattle.

2005 — The Seahawks win a team-record 13 games and reach their first Super Bowl.

2010 — Pete Carroll takes over as head coach and leads the team to the playoffs.

2013 — Quarterback Russell Wilson leads the Seahawks to their first Super Bowl title.

2014 — The Seahawks come within a yard of winning a second straight Super Bowl.

2022 — Wilson is traded to the Broncos, and Geno Smith leads the Seahawks to the playoffs.

2023 — Carroll steps down after 14 seasons as head coach.

59

COMPREHENSION QUESTIONS

Write your answers on a separate piece of paper.

1. Write a paragraph that explains the main ideas of Chapter 2.

2. Who do you think was the greatest player in Seahawks history? Why?

3. Who was the Seahawks' first starting quarterback?
   - A. Dave Krieg
   - B. Jim Zorn
   - C. Matt Hasselbeck

4. Why is crowd noise helpful to the home team?
   - A. Noise makes it harder for the opponents to hear the play call.
   - B. Noise makes the opponents excited to play hard.
   - C. Noise makes the home team know what play to run.

5. What does **anchored** mean in this book?

*He **anchored** the defensive line for 11 seasons. Kennedy earned the Defensive Player of the Year Award in his third season.*

    A. scored many points

    B. failed in a big way

    C. led with talent

6. What does **controversial** mean in this book?

*It was a **controversial** game. The officials later admitted to mistakes that hurt the Seahawks.*

    A. not likely to make a difference

    B. likely to be argued about

    C. likely to be forgotten

Answer key on page 64.

GLOSSARY

conference
A group of teams that make up part of a sports league.

division
In the NFL, a group of teams that make up part of a conference.

drafted
Selected a new player coming into the league.

expansion team
A new team that is added to a league.

interception
A pass that is caught by a defensive player.

playoffs
A set of games played after the regular season to decide which team is the champion.

sacks
Plays that happen when a defender tackles the quarterback before he can throw the ball.

scrambling
Running around behind the line of scrimmage to avoid pass rushers.

secondary
The defensive players, such as cornerbacks and safeties, who start the play farthest from the line of scrimmage.

seismograph
An instrument that measures and records details of earthquakes.

TO LEARN MORE

BOOKS

Coleman, Ted. *Seattle Seahawks All-Time Greats.* Mendota Heights, MN: Press Room Editions, 2022.

Kawa, Katie. *Russell Wilson: Making a Difference as a Quarterback.* New York: KidHaven Publishing, 2023.

Klepeis, Alicia. *Seattle Seahawks.* Minneapolis: Bellwether Media, 2024.

ONLINE RESOURCES

Visit **www.apexeditions.com** to find links and resources related to this title.

ABOUT THE AUTHOR

Brendan Flynn is a San Francisco resident and an author of numerous children's books. In addition to writing about sports, Flynn also enjoys competing in triathlons, Scrabble tournaments, and chili cook-offs.

INDEX

Alexander, Shaun, 27

Brown, Dave, 24

Carroll, Pete, 30
Chancellor, Kam, 45

Diggs, Quandre, 46

Easley, Kenny, 24

Green, Jacob, 24

Hasselbeck, Matt, 27
Holmgren, Mike, 14, 16

Jones, Walter, 27

Kennedy, Cortez, 24, 28
Knox, Chuck, 12
Krieg, Dave, 20

Largent, Steve, 18, 20, 53
Lockett, Tyler, 43
Lynch, Marshawn, 40, 55

Metcalf, D. K., 43

Rice, Jerry, 53

Sherman, Richard, 45
Smith, Geno, 37

Thomas, Earl, 45

Wagner, Bobby, 46
Walker, Kenneth, III, 43
Warner, Curt, 22
Wilson, Russell, 32, 35, 37, 38, 40, 43
Woolen, Riq, 45

Zorn, Jim, 20

ANSWER KEY:
1. Answers will vary; 2. Answers will vary; 3. B; 4. A; 5. C; 6. B